T0113591

When 40 is NOT ENOUGH

rJo Winch

Order this book online at www.trafford.com
or email orders@trafford.com

Most Trafford titles are also available at major online book retailers.

© Copyright 2021 rJo Winch.
All rights reserved. No part of this publication may be reproduced, stored in a
retrieval system, or transmitted, in any form or by any means, electronic, mechanical,
photocopying, recording, or otherwise, without the written prior permission of the author.

Print information available on the last page.

ISBN: 978-1-6987-0672-6 (sc)
ISBN: 978-1-6987-0673-3 (e)

Because of the dynamic nature of the Internet, any web addresses or links contained in
this book may have changed since publication and may no longer be valid. The views
expressed in this work are solely those of the author and do not necessarily reflect the
views of the publisher, and the publisher hereby disclaims any responsibility for them.

Any people depicted in stock imagery provided by Getty Images are models, and such
images are being used for illustrative purposes only.
Certain stock imagery © Getty Images.

Trafford rev. 05/21/2021

www.trafford.com
North America & international
toll-free: 844-688-6899 (USA & Canada)
fax: 812 355 4082

DEDICATION

To my mother Prenzina Holloway; Lifelong community activist; member of the 1st and 7th Districts Hartford Democratic Town Committee; 1st Black Women Deputy Sheriff of Hartford County.

To my children, thank you for just being there. No matter what I go through, you are there with your unconditional love and patience.

To my sibling, you always have my back, I love you.

THE FOREWORD

This story was born four years prior to the 2015 City of Hartford municipal election. What happened in 2011 at the Hartford Democratic Town Committee (HDTC) Convention set in motion the foundation of the words printed on these pages.

Within these pages is the desire to help others understand local government, how it works, and what people can do to influence change where they live. What you are about to learn applies no matter what city, town, rural area or suburb people reside within these Unites States of America. Let's just say my desire is to help others unlock the door to their local government by being enlightened to what you can do when the stakes are high, and the odds are against you.

Within these pages are the endless possibilities available to any candidate when the people they love, trust and dedicate their life to help turn their backs on them and they find a bond with someone they never thought would be in there corner because just four short years prior, they too were on the other side. Thus, the political phrase of, "No permanent enemies," is proven to be true.

Because I considered the task before me was so hard, so unattainable and so high, I compared it to mountain climbing for the first time. Through my experience I want to help open your eyes and help you learn there are many techniques needed to overcome the fears of climbing an unclimbable mountain; realizing you will be entering into unchartered territory; there is no need to be fearful. When I began this journey, I was a novice at the game of mountain climbing too.

As a matter of fact, I had several failed attempts. But because I was tireless and unwilling to give up, I kept trying until I discovered what held the mountain together and I began to chisel at the sides, chipping away one rock at a time.

Every fallen rock represented another lesson learned. I kept learning and reaching out for more knowledge from those who thought to climb this mountain but gave up, anticipating they would fail. Their failures became my foundation.

CHAPTER ONE

To have a clear understanding of this journey, I have to take you back to the year of 2011 at the Hartford Democratic Town Committee (HDTC) Convention, in the month of July, where the task was to endorse the City of Hartford Democratic candidates for Mayor, City Council, City Treasurer and Constable. This convention took place every four years and its membership consists of about 70 town committee members. Which meant each endorsed candidate needed to acquire at least 50% plus one (36) votes.

It began as most conventions do, with the roll call of members present. Our convention consists of six districts: Districts: 1st, 3rd, 4th, 5th, 6th and 7th. There was no 2nd District because the City of Hartford lost that district after the 2010 CENSUS which also led to a redistricting.

First on the agenda was the nominations for Mayor which was a pretty smooth process. There was one other candidate that was running for Mayor but there was not much support for changing that office to someone new. Everyone seemed to have made an agreement that the sitting Mayor would be endorsed to continue in the office he currently held. As each town committee member was called, they cast their votes for their selection. When the roll call ended the sitting Mayor was the HDTC Endorsed Democratic Candidate for Mayor.

Second, on the agenda was nominations for the Court of Common Council, aka City Council. During this process was where I made my first of many mistakes. I was under the impression that everyone was fair and that all could be trusted. I found out that was a misconception on my part. Therefore, I did not discriminate who I held conversations with. When I had meetings, no matter what the subject; all were welcome to attend. I did not take the time to ensure plans did not make their way out of the room. I trusted when the group said information was not to leave the room, it didn't. How wrong I was; misconception number 2.

The night before the Hartford Democratic Town Committee Convention, a group of us met, as we had done almost weekly with two other districts hoping to put together an alliance that would land our candidates with endorsements for Hartford City Council.

The group of us met for about 6 weeks only to have that relationship building go to hell, at the convention, in a matter of seconds. How? I'm glad you asked. One of the nights we met, the 4th District Candidate for City Treasurer unexpectantly showed up to our meeting. I should say, unexpected to some of us, because the person who invited him knew we were meeting and obviously ask him to come and ask the group of us for our support for his endorsement. Because all of us had basically already committed our votes to the sitting Treasurer it was hard to move the votes to him at this late date. I guess to that, he was not happy, and he abruptly left the dinner prior to us finishing our discussion.

I thought nothing more of it until the night of the convention. The minute the uninvited City Treasurer candidate from the 4th District approached one of the districts for support and was told they had already committed their votes to his opponent he and his district members pulled their votes away from me and in return my district pulled all of their votes from their candidate who I and several other members of the 7th were working with to build a citywide coalition. This meant although I was the current sitting Council President, I would not receive enough votes to be endorsed at this convention.

After that played out, all I could do was sit in the audience with the look of disgust, realizing this meant I was more than likely not going to get the HDTC endorsement for City Council.

Fuming mad, I just sat and watched the rest of the convention take place. Once the first round of votes ended, they had endorsed six men to represent the Endorsed Democrats for Hartford City Council. For a moment I actually thought I also received enough votes for the endorsement because my number read 37. This year the goal was 35.

Strangely, when I looked up again, it was 31. Not sure how that happened because I did not hear anyone making changes to their votes, but anyway.

Once it was all said and done the committee moved on to endorse the City Treasurer.

I make mention of the Endorsed Council member's gender only because there were four women also running for the city council endorsement and not one woman was endorsed in a city where the largest voting block, no matter what district anyone lived in was women.

That night ended around 2:00am the next morning, with several unendorsed candidates, including myself, met to try and put a slate together to challenge the endorsed slate. We soon realized making that happen was utterly impossible. This slate would have comprised of people who had almost nothing in common. There was too much bad blood between us to be resolved in such a short time to allow us to run a successful campaign. The reality was that even if we managed to put a slate together and happen to win by a landslide, we would not be a governing body.

By the next day as emotions died down, we agreed that this was not going to work. Some decided to let it go while some of us set out to challenge the endorsed

Democrats on our own with people other than those in the room.

After this disappointing evening I returned to the Tuesday night group with a new mandate. If I was to challenge the endorsed Democrats, I would need their help. The Tuesday night group was a group of community activist who met at a particular club and discussed everything to include business ventures, religion and politics. Three of us who were not endorsed attended these meetings. Two of us were Democrats and one a Republican. Not being endorsed meant to have access to the ballot a candidate would have to obtain over 2,500 signatures from registered democrats within 10 days. The candidate for Mayor decided he would go it alone. That left me and the other two candidates to make an important decision to how we would go forward.

At the next Tuesday night meeting we decided to put together a challenge slate, thinking everyone would help us get the required signatures to get our names on the ballot. Little did I know, at the time, some people at the meeting were double agents.

As we continued to meet every Tuesday night, I continued to share information and assist each of the candidates with their campaigns to include collecting signatures. I set up training sessions with their volunteers, explained the process to them and followed up with them as if I was the campaign manager for them as well as myself.

As the signatures came in, I checked each sheet to be sure they would count. I actually requested no one turn in their signatures to the Hartford Democratic Registrar's Office until they were verified as democratic registered voters. We did not have time to come up short. We had to collect these signatures to have access to the ballot. So, it was crucial that every signature be valid.

As more signatures came in, I started noticing the first five on every page was the same people. Some of the volunteers helping us thought it a great idea to give us repeat signatures. This surely did not help. It did not make much sense to give us signatures that we already counted. They could not be counted more than once. This was a valuable lesson for me about the integrity of some volunteers. I realize not everyone is outgoing and easy to knock on a stranger's door to ask for their support and signatures. But I could not appreciate their dishonesty, so I quickly dismissed these individuals and doubled my own efforts to collect signatures because their shenanigans had cost us valuable time by causing us to recheck signatures I had already confirmed. Furthermore, these would not count in our total number of signatures we needed to collect to obtain access to the ballot, so these volunteers had to go.

Now that we lost about 40 signatures which is two pages, and the time is shorter, we had to accelerate our rate of collection. At our next Tuesday night meeting I gave an update on how many signatures were collected, how much time we had, and how many more were needed. Considering the time remaining and how much work was still needed I called upon those unconditional, always there supporters called; my family. I pulled in every registered democrat in my family and my newly established friends to help get signatures because we had come too far to come up short.

This was a group I could trust and there was no need to double check behind them but because of the practices of a few, I checked any way. To my amazement when I received a call from the

Democratic Registrar of Voters, not only had they collected the signatures in record time, but they far exceeded the number of signatures required. By the time they finished, we had over 3,000 signatures when we only needed 2,500 on the city side and more than 300 which was required on the State signature sheets for a petitioning candidate for the November ballot just in case, I lost the primary with the slate.

Now that we had the signatures in, we could concentrate on door knocking, collecting donations, ordering lawn signs and phone banking. The most important of these is door knocking. This is where we actually got an opportunity to meet and greet the voters where they live.

At the following Tuesday night weekly meeting I brought in literature that I had created which included each of our photos along with where we were on the ballot. I had prepared a list of voting residents and their addresses and put them in clear plastic bags. We sat around the table and stuffed the bags and discussed sending out a mailer of the same to those who lived in apartment buildings since we had no other way of reaching them since we could not get into their buildings to knock on their doors.

One of the people, who shall remain nameless, but if he reads this chapter will know it is him, left with one of our flyers. I thought nothing of it until a few days later I received that same literature created by the endorsed slate in my mailbox.

I was heated and called the co-chair of the Tuesday night meeting group and expressed my displeasure in what had happened. He thought it was okay and we should press on with our plans. I felt differently about it and began to be more cautious about the information I shared with them and retracted on what steps would lead us all to victory. I started to realize some who came to the meeting were not there for us. They only came to gather information to share with our opponents.

Over time the other candidates were convinced by outsiders that they would win their races for council if they separated themselves from me. They went as far as wanting to meet in a hiding place so their other supporters would not know we were meeting. This was quite childish, and I told them so, *"I'm not in high school and I don't need to hide who I do business with."*

This is when I realized this was not a team effort. They proved to be self-serving individuals running for the position of City Council, with too many outside alliances.

Needless to say, as a result of not working as a team, the Endorsed Democrats won all six seats during the primary. As I challenged them for the general election, I also did not win. This was where I learned another lesson about mountain climbing.

So, for the next four years, I build relationships with people they did not know, met with unconditional supporters, and made my own way outside of the group. I met with HDTC members on my own. I partnered with youth organizations and kept by focus on building relationships with Neighborhood Revitalization Zone members and got involved in community business outside of the Tuesday night group.

I continued to not share what I was doing or my motivation behind it. I could feel that my relationship with some of the group members was trending downward. I noticed that less people were showing up and there was less comradery amongst the remaining group members. In essence, the group dynamics were starting to deteriorate. Some of them shared unfortunate circumstances that had nothing to do with the group or me. They just happened to be members of another club and their feelings toward each other filtered over into this group. However, bad as it was their underlying issues had nothing to do with me nor where I wanted to go. I was aware of them and they started to affect others in attendance to the point they stopped attending. I felt bad but I was not going to get in between what I called other people's issues. I had a few issues of my own to be resolved and I was on my 2015 endorsement mission. I was not going to be distracted by other business I could not resolve if I had the desire to try. I had fish to fry and relationships to mend or rebuilt. I was not about to let anything stop me from climbing this mountain.

One person I always had a great relationship with was Linda King-Corbin. She was someone I met during my first term on Hartford City Council when I served as the First Female and First Black Councilmember to serve as Council President. We both attended Phillips CME Church here in the City of Hartford on Main Street. She was on the Trustee Board and a member of the Nurses' Guild while I served on their Usher Board. She was also the spouse of the Department of Public's Works Director which I found out about that connection later when I just happened to ask if they were related. That had nothing to do with our relationship, I just mentioned it to reiterate that Hartford is a small place and without looking for it you will soon discover that most of us have some type of connection, be it work related, religious or personal.

So anyway, she was one of those members who started pulling away from the Tuesday night group before me. I did not understand at the time, but now realized she, as I did, found the group to no longer be as beneficial as it was when we started several years back.

She also introduced me to the Kiwanis International Club, which is an outstanding youth group that has been in existed for more than 130 years. It is an organization that I'd never heard of with all of the work they do assisting youth in high school and through college. I was glad to be a part of this group and found them and their members to be very supportive and committed to their mission of engaging more multi-cultural members to diversify their organization.

While the Kiwanis is not political the members are honest and dedicated. I appreciated them for that. I also came to know another dedicated friend named Victor Luna. I mention these two friends by name because their support was vital to my mountain climb. I never told them how much they mean to me or how their friendships helped me, as they continued to be honest, supportive and upfront with me even when we had political disagreements. No matter what the politics, we were able to separate that from our friendship. I greatly appreciated that about them considering they were also from the Tuesday night group. Whenever I needed assistance, they made themselves available with no questions asked. I intern continued to do the same. These two are my ride or die friends.

Were it not for their friendships I don't know how I would have found the strength to continue this fight. But I kept telling myself, *"I am on a mission to succeed and I cannot fail."*

With Linda, Vic and my Pastor on my side I felt invincible. I needed to succeed for them as well as myself. I did not want their friendship to be wasted on a loser. I kept them closely informed when I was not talking to anyone else. I continued to volunteer my services and kept building relationships with people I had come in contact with and did not share any of them or their information with the Tuesday night group.

By this time, I figured this Tuesday night group were too loose with the lips and nothing I shared there was sacred. I had to regroup my thinking when it came to the group and keep a lot to myself. So even when I continued to attend, I was quietly planning in the back of my mind and not sharing what I was planning with anyone, hoping that this strategy would pay off and land me where I was going in 2015.

For the next three years I was like a stealth bomber, not letting anyone know what I was doing by way of politics. I kept my relationships close and those who did not have a need to know didn't. It's not because they did not ask, it was because I was not sharing when they asked.

CHAPTER TWO

Fast forwarding to the year of 2015. One of my New Year's resolutions was to shed all of the backstabbing, non-supporters and start building a team of people whom I could trust. It did not make a difference to me if they were ever involved in politics or if they knew a Democrat from a Republican. I needed a team of individuals who were unconditionally with me. I needed an army of committed people I could count on no matter who we were up against. The only thing that was important at this moment was that they knew our mission was to make sure rJo Winch was elected in 2015 to the Hartford City Council by way of the Hartford Democratic Town Committee (HDTC) Endorsement.

I'd had enough of those fake people with double alliances and no allegiance to me. When anyone I approached for support said, *"I like you, but I also want to support so and so,"* I quickly told them to go and support them because I had played that game before and it did not work out for me. Whenever this conversation took place, I mentally dropped them from my list of supporters and put them on the average voter list. After having a conversation with one of these types of supporters, I politely gave him a ride to the other candidate's house.

I had been taught another valuable lesson from people like him and now when I conducted my meetings, not one person who wanted to work with another candidate other than rJo Winch was invited to the table. I had no intention of repeating what happened to me in 2011. I was so in the zone, I actually dumped all of my so-called friends and fake associates and started building new relationships and new alliances. Yes, they could have proven to be another mistake, but I knew I could not trust those I trusted the last time, so I was willing to take a chance on those who I knew were upfront and those who were new.

Months leading up to the July 27th, 2015 Hartford Democratic Town Committee Convention, my Spokesperson/Campaign Manager and I met with every town committee member in all 6 HDTC Districts. We met often with supporters she knew, and I also met with some she didn't. I did not share them with her because I needed to protect the security of their votes and sometimes not sharing is helpful when you are on a one time take all mission that could not withstand a miss. This one was it and playing smart was the game and winning had to be the outcome.

Remember I told you one of my New Year's Resolutions was to shed myself of shady people? My second one was to lead the Hartford Democratic Town Committee to where they ended up around 1:30am on the morning of July 28th. The last time I was seeking their endorsement they had around 70 members. Through signature collection and the redistricting some were awarded additional members and now they were at 78.

My goal was still 50% plus one. Which meant, since they had been increased to 78 HDTC members, I needed to get 50% plus one of them to endorse me to even have a chance at winning a seat to serve on council. For easy math, that is 39 plus 1. An even 40 was what I thought I needed. Therefore, I set my sights on getting a simple majority plus one.

I thought that was going to be easy, but it was not as easy or as simple as one might think. I was trusting my Spokesperson to help me keep score while many around kept asking the question, *"How much do you trust your Spokesperson?"*

The 1st District Democratic Town Committee was where I started. After the 2010 Census the City of Hartford was redistricted, and the 1st, 5th, and 7th Districts were merged to make one. It was important now more than ever for me to get them on board. The year I was running for re-election by way of this endorsement there were 21 people running for 6 seats on the Democratic Council Endorsed Slate.

The 1st district was my new home after the redistricting merger. I had been in the 7th District for many years and now I am in the 1st without relocating from my current home. The members of the 1st were now my new HDTC members and I needed a solid 15 out of 15 of them to say they would cast their votes to endorse me before I could move forward. It just did not make sense to ask other districts to endorse me if my own would not.

Some of them were hard to move because they belonged to the same district as someone else running for Council who came from their former district and every candidate was looking for no less than 40 members out of the 76 to seal their endorsement.

This person who shall remain nameless was the reason some said they were not sure they could or would endorse me. This back-and-forth phone calling went on for weeks. I could recall some members from the 1st and some other districts entertaining my conversation while others were still holding out and waiting for the decision of their District Spokesperson prior to making any commitments to me.

The candidate they were waiting on did not do any of the preliminary work that most of us had done. Things like sending a request letter for endorsement to all HDTC members, regardless to what district they lived in. Most candidates prepared a cover sheet, sent resumes' and lastly participated in an open forum interview process with each town committee district.

I did not mind being realigned because most of us already knew each other and we had past political relationships with one another when I belonged to the 7th District. I must admit, not every relationship with each of them was a good one. Many of the members still had issues with me when I was on City Council from 2004 to 2011 because I had beat them in contested elections for the same office, not once, but twice.

Nonetheless, I had put those things aside a long time ago and hoped they were adult enough to do the same. I didn't have much success with many of them because the unfortunate reality is with politics, there is that set of people who you come across that will hate you for the rest of their lives because you did not see eye to eye with them on any one issue.

One such person in the 1st District always made it a point to bring up the fact that I beat him on multiple occasions. This let me know he was not willing to let that go. He made that very clear to me because he continued to bring it up 10 years later at almost at every 1st District Town Committee meeting. I guess beating me must be on his bucket list. For that reason alone, some the members still wanted to punish me for something I had no control over. Things like having the protection of my old slate members who understood commitment to one another. Rather we agreed 100% or not we moved as a team. We ironed out our differences in meetings or at the caucus. We did not air our disagreements in public. This was never discussed. It was just the underlying understanding that we shared to move as a democratic unit. For this some called us bobble heads. This could have not been further from the truth. It was this understanding of not coming out against one another that lead to these types of people thinking we were spineless or did not have an educated clue to what was going on around us. They thought we just said yes to whatever the administration wanted without asking questions. I personally was never asked to do anything for one side of the city that I did not request something for the side of the city to which I resided. It was also understood that this is how things got done. If a Councilmember or the Mayor wanted an initiative done for their constituents, before anyone could respond, the question was asked, *"What would it take for you to say yes on this project or initiative?"* There was always a platform for negotiation.

I think those on the outside of this relationship did not understand this dynamic and so I continue to be punished because they could not set aside their differences with Mayor Perez, the city's first Latino Mayor, who was cunning enough to get the HDTC members to endorse me. A position I never thought I would be in because just 2 short years prior to that endorsement I was the treasurer for his opponent. I always said this spoke to his character, that he was able to put that aside and trust that I would be committed to our new slate. He was right and I did, thanks to my military training where we normally rededicated ourselves to new leadership almost every three years. So, making this transition was easy. I was also very new to the political arena as a candidate, although I had helped with others whenever I was home on leave from the military. There were also two other candidates running with me at the time who did not participate in the process, but he managed to get the HDTC to endorse them too.

I failed to understand how their issues with him became my issues. I had just retired and returned home from the United States Air Force and ended up in the middle the most significant historical election in the City of Hartford. It was the year the Mayor of the City of Hartford was to become the first strong Mayor under the new City Charter voted on by the residents of Hartford.

I was ready to let the past be in the past. However, I did not have the fortune of them doing the same. Too many of them still could not put whatever differences they had with me on the back burner and press on. I still look at their attitudes as too elementary for me. They reminded me of elementary school with what I called playground behavior. I did not and still do not have brain cells to harbor such childishness.

But, fortunately and unfortunately, for me, my new district is historically where most of our local elected officials reside. The current and immediate past endorsed Democratic Mayor, three Council members and the City Treasurer all lived in the 1st District. If I was to receive their support I had to learn to adapt to this dynamic. Although I found it quite different from the last team of councilmembers, where we just clicked. While difficult for sure, it was what I had to do to be given an opportunity to work for my constituents and make changes for the residents I hoped to serve as their Councilwoman.

CHAPTER THREE

So here we are in January 2015 and it is time to elect the new 1st District Democratic Town Committee. This is a process that takes place every two years in the City of Hartford. However, the process was a little different this year because of the 2010 CENSUS. This year the process consisted of current town committee members coming to a scheduled meeting and expressing their desire to be on the town committee or not.

Having been invited to the meeting, I naively thought we were all on the same page, only to find out in a matter of minutes we were not. Some of the merged members of the town committee were still angry about the merger, but we could not do anything about that. I personally felt like I was looked upon as an outsider because I was currently not a member of any town committee although I had previously served on the 7th District.

This meeting consisted of members who currently served on the 1st, 5th and 7th Districts of the HDTC. This was the time scheduled to ask if anyone wanted to remain on the town committee. There were 15 people who could be on the list and each one had to sign the form which put them on the 1st District slate.

The list went around the room and everyone present said if they chose to continue on the 1st District Town Committee or make room for those from the 5th or the 7th District. Those who wanted to continue signed the form. This was of course until the form came around to me. When I attempted to sign the form, I was abruptly stopped as someone said, *"Hold up. What about Prenzina?"*

Prenzina Holloway, is my mother and she, having been a lifelong member of the town committee, it was respectful of them to inquire if she wanted to continue as a town committee member in our new district prior to letting me sign the form.

Since she was currently a member of the 7th District Town Committee, it was the right thing to do. She being a current member had priority to remain a member but, on the 1st, instead of the 7th.

So, prior to the completion of the form, I was given the task of having a conversation with my mother to see if she would step down for me to take her place on the town committee. I immediately got an attitude and kindly removed myself from the room because I was not about to let them put me against my own mother for a town committee seat. I thought they should have had that conversation prior to inviting me to attend the meeting.

Anyway, the answer to that question was a no brainer for me. I already knew if my mother said she wanted the seat, she could have it and I would be satisfied to be her proxy.

When I returned home, I called mom and explained what had happened at the meeting. I expressed to her that evidently, we both could not be on the town committee or at least, that was what I gathered from their conversation. I assumed they did not want both of us to be on the same town committee, although the Spokesperson and her mom were both on there.

However, if she wanted to have the seat it was hers. I was pleased to yield the seat to her. She intern said if I wanted it, I could have it and she would yield to me. I continued to explain that I would only take it if she really did not want to be a part of the HDTC any longer. She assured me that she was getting tired and did not want to put in the time and go to all of the scheduled meetings, but she would agree to be my proxy whenever I was unable to be present. To that I agreed, and I asked her to call our Spokesperson and inform her of what she had decided to do about the Town Committee seat.

That very next day our Spokesperson called me with the news I already knew and later that evening she stopped by my house for me to sign as the last remaining signature on the form.

The next step in the process was to collect signatures from registered voters. This was a task that should be completed by everyone on the slate. All 15 members were given pages to be signed by registered Democratic voters who live in the 1st District. Each member on the slate was to go out in our district, knock on voters' doors and get them to sign their forms.

This was no easy task because it was January in New England and this year January was brutally cold, and to add fuel to the fire, it was also raining most of the days, which turned into ice as night fell upon us. But that did not stop those of us who were dedicated from going out every day and collecting signatures for our slate.

We needed to collect 300 signatures in about 10 days. Unlike other districts we did not have a challenge slate against us so collecting the correct number of signatures would be considered our votes to be on the 1st District Town Committee. While other districts had to collect signatures and have an actual election in March of this same year; we escaped this part of the process by joining forces.

Fortunately, our Spokesperson and I went out every day, in the cold rain and snow, knocking on doors until our district had collected more than 400 signatures. We wanted them to be collected on time and be sure that we had 300 good signatures for our 1st District Democratic Town Committee slate. Day after day we sacrificed our wellbeing while other people on the same slate either did not go out at all or collected less than 20 signatures to assist us with the 300 signatures we needed to qualify. I thought it not fair, but I was accustomed to these types of people considering how we had to collect signature when I ran in 2011 and lost that race. The same thing happened during our slate signature collection. While some of us worked others just reaped the benefit of our work.

While out in the cold collecting signatures, I got so sick I thought I had pneumonia. I was so sick, but the need was there and when my Spokesperson called and said she received word from the Registrar that we were short she called and several of us went out to get a few more signatures to be sure that we would qualify and avoid an election in March.

Nonetheless, we collected over 400 signatures and understood that if by some chance we lost 100 of them because sometimes people were lazy and instead of getting registered voters from the list they were given, they would let anyone sign and in this case every signature had to be registered voters who lived in the 1st District.

CHAPTER FOUR

January ended and February was upon us. As other districts were preparing and campaigning for the March election, we were all done, and our signatures had been certified by the Democratic Registrar of Voters.

Now it was time to start calling those district town committee members who did not have a challenge and ask them if they would consider giving me their endorsement for Hartford City Council and the obvious place for me to start was with my own district. When I did, I made an interesting discovery.

I discovered by accident that my Spokesperson was also a candidate for City Council. This was shocking to me because while she said she was calling other Town Committee members on my behalf; one has to wonder if she was really calling them for me or for herself. How did I find out? I'm glad you asked. As I made my calls to town committee members several of them asked me the question: *"How can you and your Spokesperson be both running for Hartford City Council? How can she cut a deal for both of you?"*

One member had the nerve to say, *"Why don't you get out of the Council race and get appointed as the new Democratic Registrar after the election?"*

As if that was an option. That would be the biggest long shot ever. Why would I give up what I want to make a bet on getting something that was utterly impossible as that? Furthermore, all Registrar of Voters are elected positions in the City of Hartford. and why would I bet on such a long shot from a council I don't know.

I figured this person is confused or thinking I am stupid and would go for this idea and give up my chance for receiving the endorsement. I guess they did not know the Council appoints the Town Clerk and not the Registrars.

So, I paid not much attention to that nonsense. However, it did give me reason to concern myself with my Spokesperson. Must have been some truth to her running because there had to be a reason this subject kept coming up.

I'll just park that in the parking lot for now. Every time someone asked me that I did not let on to them that I was surprised by their question. I just said I was calling for myself. I assumed she was calling for herself. I can imagine that left them quite confused to have both of us asking for their support. It made me wonder if their hesitation in making a commitment to me was the mixed messages that were being sent by other 1st District Town Committee members or our Spokesperson. I assume some of them wanted to support her while others said they would definitely support me, but they did not want to cause any issues within the District, which I clearly understood. They were a cohesive group. Only a few others and I were new to the team.

I continued to make calls and ignored that conversation for the moment although the question of my new Spokesperson also running for the same office without saying a word about it to me could be the reason for their apprehension.

That means she knew why I was having an issue as I shared my numbers with her. However, she made no mention of her numbers or that she was advocating for the endorsement for herself. And we talked often so there was plenty of time to bring this up.

One might ask, how can she call herself working on my behalf as my Spokesperson/Campaign Manager and be also running herself? This subject also came up at one of the Tuesday night meetings where, for the first time I heard her say, out loud, that she was not running for the council endorsement.

I guess what she really meant to say was she was not running anymore, cause surely unrelated people had told me and others, she was asking them for support for her run. Although I heard what she said, I was no longer comfortable with her calling for me. I started making those calls to other town committee members for myself. I felt betrayed as I talked to some of them. Not by them, but by her not having talked to them and not saying a word about what was going on.

Of course, I was not happy. Actually, I was quite embarrassed. Finally, I had to confront her and instructed her to tell the other town committee members, she was not running or tell me to my face that she is so I can make other arrangements for a new Campaign Manager. By the way, I never asked her to be my Campaign Manager, this was a position she took on.

After many days of calling for endorsement support, she finally told the Tuesday night group she was definitely not running. Although that was great news to hear it did not leave the members of the Tuesday night group with a comfortable feeling about her because they knew the work, I put in to help her when she wanted to run for Democratic Registrar of Voters.

I actually organized and hosted a campaign fundraiser for her at the club. I was there for her without question. I thought we were just that close. However, her run for Democratic Registrar fell through; not because of me, but because the support she needed was not there for her election to this office. So, when I found out she was running for the same office as me I felt like she stabbed me in the back.

After several meetings when she said out of her own mouth that she was absolutely not running for City Council, we moved on but very cautiously from that moment forward. I placed this incident in the parking lot. Where is the parking lot? This is the space in the back of my mind that I store thoughts I may need to recall. just in case I may need to act on them later. I put thoughts in the parking lot, so I don't forget them. I know where they are and I can access them, at will, at the appropriate time. Some people refer to this area as their memory bank.

CHAPTER FIVE

When March came and the other Democratic Town Committee Districts elections were over, I could now start calling the winners and ask them for their support. I was hoping I no longer had to have that conversation about my Spokesperson running. I also felt there should have been overwhelming support for me from the 7th District where I had lived until the redistricting took place.

I surprisingly found out their support was contingent on my new district's support for their two candidates. So that meant my support was not etched in stone even though I was almost single handedly responsible for the majority of these members being on this town committee. Their Chair of the Neighborhood Revitalization Zone (NRZ) and I worked on behalf of their slate. She went to City

Hall and got their paperwork for them. We met at a neighborhood bookstore where we showed them how to complete the paperwork and she took the paperwork back to city hall so they could get their forms to go out and collect signatures to have access to the ballot, only to have them after the election, give control of their town committee back to the people they just won against.

I could not believe it when I heard about their first leadership meeting. I was puzzled and asked the question why? I was told that they wanted to give them a leadership position as good faith and show there was no animosity towards them even though they ran against them and replaced have of their old members.

This is politics 101 gone bad. You do not run a challenge slate, win the race and give the slate you beat leadership positions on the slate where you control 51% of the vote. I could not stop shaking my head on that one.

Actually, after the election in March a little more than half of them from the slate I was helping with and 8 from the challenge slate were elected to serve together. This was not caused by any of the members I assisted. The voters of the district split their votes and picked some from one slate and some from the another and thus they had to work out their differences because now they were one.

I must admit I was quite puzzled when I found out my support was contingent on their two new council candidates getting support from the 1st District Town Committee members. In other words, their support for me was now contingent on my new district's support for their two candidates. Two for one may have seemed unfair but that was the deal they were offering. Actually, it was two for two because my Spokesperson claimed she was trying to get a four-council endorsement package deal. I really did not care who I was endorsed with, I was on a mission to being endorsed; period!

And just to show you how shady people can be, when I arrived at the next Tuesday night meeting one of the candidates who was also running for City Council came there for support. I was surprised to see her because no one mentioned to me that any candidates were attending the meeting that night. Any other time we would share with one another if we had invited someone to attend just to keep people in the loop. There was no approval process. We just did it out of courtesy.

Anyway, I did and did not have a problem with her attendance. She was someone I knew from the past administration. What I also knew was that she did not arrive without an invitation. She was not that type of person to just show up without being invited. Especially since she knew I was running, and I was the Co-Chair of the group. She would not be that disrespectful.

Come to find out the other Co-Chair of the group invited her to address the group and when she was done, he pledged to give his 100% support for her candidacy. Well, I guess that meant I was getting 0% support because percentage of support normally only go up to 100%.

Not wanting to show my emotion or how embarrassed I was, we thanked her for coming and moved on with the remainder of the meeting. However, after the meeting I called the Treasurer of the group and expressed to her how angry and embarrassed I was feeling about what had happened. She expressed that she was also not pleased because she knew I had invested more than 8 years of my life to this organization and that was the thanks I got.

She expressed that she was surprised too. I told her I knew the candidate was invited by the Co-Chair. I mentioned I'd talked to her later and she was also surprised because she assumed that I had the support of the group. I did not tell her, but that made two of us.

The next Tuesday when we had the meeting, I'm sure they picked up on, how much less I was willing to share. I was almost silent on my campaign and did not request their assistance and had nothing more to share on ways they could help with the endorsement although two of our members were members of two different town committees.

However, that following Wednesday, I received a call from one of my real supporters named Rev Paul Ritter. He asked if I could meet with him and the breakfast club at McDonald's in the meadows. I was hesitant to go because some members of the breakfast club were also anti rJo supporters and people that blamed me for having a positive relationship with the former Mayor Eddie Perez.

My sentiment was I had no bearing on their past relationship. Whatever they went through with him was what I called "BR" (Before rJo). I did not know why they were upset with him and I was not going to spend one minute of my time trying to resolve irrelevant issues between two adults. It was not something I could fix, and nor did I have the time to try.

I was on a single mission. That was to get the HDTC endorsement, and nothing was going to get in my way. Not even the past baggage of relationships gone bad that had absolutely nothing to do with me.

Soon after my arrival Rev came in and we went to the counter to order our breakfast. As we did others started to come in and joined us in the line. I could tell by the looks on their faces they were surprised to see me at the Breakfast Club.

But Rev had been in my corner from the start. He was an avid supporter from the first time I ran for office and his support had not changed over the years. He was always in my corner. He was one of those Ole Gs who knew my mother and the fantastic work she had done for under privileged children in

Hartford and as far as he was concerned, I was a chip off of her block.

As the conversations moved from everyday newspaper gossip to politics, I was asked the question to what I was going to do different than I'd done the last time I was elected. My response was simple, I told them I was going to continue building relationships with our community and I would appreciate it if people would stop lumping me with others whom they had bad blood with and let me represent the residents of Hartford as rJo and not look at me through the lens of others.

Moving on from there one of the members who had also talked to the Co-Chair of the Tuesday night group said that he was willing to support me. Even though we did not always see eye to eye, he finally admitted he realized I had a hard job when it came to Union contracts and negotiation of them. He realized this was under the Mayor's control and as the Chair of Labor and Workforce all I could do was express my concerns or make recommendations and the Mayor and his administration had the final say.

He was not happy with the outcomes, but he was willing to let the issues of yesterday go and move on. As a matter of fact, a couple months after this conversation, he invited me to speak to his union for their endorsement. I was very surprised and pleased that he had done that. We had come a long way from where our relationship was prior to his retirement from the City of Hartford Department of Public Works. I will forever be grateful for his support. I know he was under a lot of pressure not to endorse me.

Another asked about the leadership of the new council. I was not really interested in this but was willing to entertain a conversation about it. It would have made much sense for me to start in leadership for the first two years and then turn it over to the next council member in line seeing that I had been there before. However, even having this conversation would be messy so I was careful about how I responded.

I did not want to go too much into details about that because it would only serve as a reason not to support me if they wanted someone else to serve in that leadership position. If anyone said I was interested that would only mucky up the waters and give some people a reason not to support me because

I was about some power grab. This was not my sentiment at all. I was on a mission to prove I had learned to climb this mountain and come July 27, 2015; I would have accomplished what I had set out to do.

CHAPTER SIX

Here we are moving into April of 2015 and I am stressing because I have yet to get to 40 HDTC votes for my endorsement. This would be the number of HDTC members who said they were willing to endorse me. By this time, I had 10 of the 15 people in my new district. The other 5 were not willing to commit for reasons they were not willing to reveal to me at this time.

When I spoke to the 3rd District, they were only willing to give 10 of their 14 votes just in case they needed the others to bargain with. I could understand that and was glad for the explanation. I was good with that and thankful for their honesty.

I figured if I was able to get the 15 from the 1st, 16 from the 7th and 13 from the 3rd, I would be all set at 44 votes. With this number I figured I could afford to lose one or two and still get the endorsement. I only got commitment for 5 from the 4th from as few faithful friends, 2 standard votes in the 5th, and 5 in the 6th who did not want to commit all of their votes for the same reasons as the 3rd. Finally, I could only get 9 of the 16 members from the 7th to commit even though, this was the town committee I almost single handedly helped to get on board.

Several months prior to the convention, they were putting forward a challenge to the existing 7th District town committee members and I helped them through the process thinking that when I needed them for an endorsement, they would undoubtedly be there. However, people in this business have short memories.

So here I sit at 36 solid votes, trying to get to 40. Although more would be great, I would be pleased just to have that many considering the confusion to which I place the blamed on my Spokesperson/ Campaign Manager, who was unbeknown**st** to me, was also trying to undercut me and get the endorsement for herself. This is what I get for trusting a snake who acted like they lost their fangs but then will silently bite you if you are not paying close attention. I guess I could think that she was trying to get votes for both of us. But that was not the conversation we had. So, if that is what she was doing it still was not a realistic goal and furthermore, that was not part of our discussion when she decided that she would advocate for me to get the HDTC endorsement. So, I was unwilling to give her the benefit of the doubt on that one.

Her actions remained steady on my mind; I never had this conversation with anyone because at this point, I was totally unsure of who I could trust outside of two members of the Tuesday night group. These two members of the group, I knew I could trust. They were always honest with me, even when we did not agree. We managed to disagree peacefully and there was not any bad blood between us because of that disagreement.

I was so unsure to what she was doing, I started having daily meeting with her to try to keep a closer eye on this process. We began to have conversations about who I should recall and who to let go now that she is claimed to be solely my campaign manager. At this point I still found it difficult to trust her because now I considered her not trustworthy. This was another issue to put in the parking lot because I was not sure when would be the next time, I would find out something that she had done, and we had not discussed it concerning my endorsement especially after that embarrassing experience.

Four years prior I trusted everyone at the table and that did not turn out in my favor. This time I was with the group but still on my own at the same time. So, as we met and talked about the campaign and what was going on, I had my committed crew to go to other locations and knock-on doors for me separately from us. Basically, I was running two campaigns. This was quite frustrating and energy draining but it was what I felt I needed to do to not leave a stone unturned.

The entire month of May was more door knocking and more town committee member calls. There were still no changes in the numbers. I actually took a break from the daily calling of town committee members and tried to raise some campaign funds. It was not easy asking for money to run a race without the HDTC endorsement. But still, I felt I was on my own. The outcome of this endorsement was totally within my control. No more was I ever going to assume work is being done. Unless I see it, I assumed it was not done and I had to do it myself.

I knew this was not going to be easy when I started because I was asking for the same people who had screwed me four years ago to now support me for re-election. A lot of nerve; you bet. This year I was convinced I could get them to endorse me. I was super determined to get support from this crew, especially because of how they treated me in 2011.

I was thankful the day the HDTC Chairman agreed to have a sit down because I knew he did not have to have a meeting with me. I appreciated him giving me the time of day. He and his dad were always emotionless; therefore, they were hard to read. But anyway, I was glad that he thought enough of me to ask my feelings about working with some of the other council candidates they had to consider. He also asked who I would not like to run with or serve with on the council.

I informed him that there was not one person I could not be elected with. I figured whom ever got elected, we would have to work together. I had no preference, and I was not about to make up one at this point. He mentioned his district normally did their own thing. He did not pressure them to support any one candidate or the other. He gave them free reign to endorse whom they pleased. This did not give me the information I needed at the time, but I was still appreciative of his honesty.

One thing I kept telling myself throughout this ordeal was that I am determined, and I was not going to give up or fail without giving it my all. This was the mountain I chose to climb and like a stray boat out on the ocean, that needed to prepare to be boarded, so did this HDTC need to be prepared for my climbed. I figured I had one last chance to make this happen and this year was it.

I knew from my military experience that a lot of actions can be measured. The one thing that no one can measure, is the determination a person has to succeed, and I was super determined to get this endorsement.

We left on cordial terms. I said I hoped his town committee was willing to give me a chance and I would do my best to be a good candidate and an even better Councilwoman.

CHAPTER SEVEN

Moving on to the month of May; I know this reads like a diary. I'm using this to help you understand the pressure of the timeline I was under to make this happen, and I don't want you to miss the timing or get lost or confused because some of these occurrences sound the same. That is because some of them are the same. However, they took place at different times during this stressful process.

As I was getting closer to to the HDTC convention I was still feeling frantic because I still could not count pass 36. I also started going to the different agencies and asking them for their financial support or their endorsements to show I had support from several organizations to include unions. Some stated they were waiting until after the convention, while others had already committed to other candidates. Some actually said, come back if you get the town committee endorsement and then we will endorse you too. Some informed me that they normally go with the town committee endorsements. Because most unions are state wide, so were their endorsements. After they had concluded all of their interviews, they would put out their state endorsements which meant they had to wait until each town had conducted their conventions.

I could not believe it but there was only one union that was willing to endorse me before anyone else. That was thanks to one of the Tuesday night meeting group members. He was a member of that union for many years, and he made calls to them for me. His advocacy landed me the endorsement and he also managed to acquire a few checks from the members too. I was so encouraged that I used this excitement to reach out to others because now I could say I had the endorsement of this Union.

From there I solicited the support of the Connecticut Childcare Provider's Union. I was sure they would endorse me after all of the work I and the bargaining team had done freely on behalf of them prior to them obtaining union status and a contract with benefits from the State of Connecticut.

I thought this would be an automatic endorsement only to find out it wasn't. After all I was a childcare provider and union member. But as I have learned through these experiences; I cannot go on what I think. I needed to have patience and believe the process would be in my favor.

I was glad they did not disappoint me. After all of the interviews from all of the competing candidates who were running that year, they put out their list of endorsed candidates across the State of Connecticut. Guess who was on the list? Yours truly. I was ecstatic when I received the postcard in my mailbox. I could not wait until the next meeting to say thanks. I called the director personally and thanked her for their support.

The next time the Childcare Provider's met was on the third Saturday of the month. When given an opportunity to address them, I thanked them for their support.

Throughout the month, it was more meetings, gatherings, collaborations and house calls. I felt so out of place at most of these meetings for more reasons than one. One reason was because I was untrusting of my new district members, but I was still unwilling to give in. I was also the only person in the room who did not consume alcoholic beverages. I did not mind that they drank, it was just sometimes they got loose lips and said things I knew they would not remember in the morning.

Having been divorced from an alcoholic I knew it was useless to try to talk to them the next day, so I just blew it off. I have been a nonalcoholic beverage drinker from way back. This was the lifestyle I took up while serving in the military. I was a Master Military Training Instructor (Drill Sergeant) which represented only 10% of the entire Air Force and like politicians' people were always looking at your life through a fine-tooth comb. I dare not give them a reason to tarnish by career choice which was not easy to come by.

I chose this career field to have an opportunity to change the lives of those who dared to enter military life. I wanted that opportunity to help them change their lives the way my Drill Instructors had pushed me to succeed. I understood my instructors played a large part of who I had become, and I wanted that for every Airman that passed through my doors.

That new beginning on life was what I wanted for others and getting in trouble with loose lips was not ever going to be my downfall. I had seen this play out with too many Air Force members who ended their military careers because of something they said while at a bar or club and were confronted about it the next day and they truly said they did not or could not remember what they had said but they were still held accountable for it because other people present heard them say it. I was sure I did not want to be like one of those people, especially in this new environment where I already did not have the trust level that I could let my guard down.

This was but one of many lessons confirmed by former Mayor Eddie Perez, who was also a nonalcoholic drinker. He always said it is important to be sober so that people cannot say you said what you know you did not say after a night of drinking.

During our term, he and I were the most sober people in the room, at any given moment and I was glad about it. I never asked him why he did not drink, I was just glad I was not alone in my decision not to. At this point after many meetings, many interviews and deal making, 40 still seemed to be a million votes away.

CHAPTER EIGHT

When we moved into June and I still did not have 40 votes, I began to really get nervous. I kept saying to myself, I cannot do this again, something has got to give. I called my Spokesperson and told her where I was with my numbers and asked her what she was doing to make sure I could get to 40. Her comments were that she was working on it. I, of course, was not happy with that and asked which districts she was working on.

She told me about the trouble she was still having in the 7th because of their two candidates. I was puzzled to what that had to do with me. They had two candidates and we had three. She said she was trying to work out the details so that four of us could get the endorsement. At least that is what she told me. But you know by this time I am very skeptical about any information I get from her because of everything that had happened up until this point. Actually, we had three candidates from the 1st District. So, if she was working on two; which two was she working on?

At our next weekly 1st District meeting in June certain candidates' names came up and we discussed them. I confirmed that I was not concerned with who my slate mates were, just as long as my name was amongst them. As we ate dinner and continued to talk politics, I asked members who were present who had not committed yet, who they were supporting. One told me straight out that they were supporting these 5 certain candidates and that they were leaning toward me for their sixth person. He had no idea how that made me feel and I did not express it. I just moved on into the room to talk to another member. He said yes rJo you are one of us and we all should be supporting you. I did not know what that meant, and I was not asking. I decided to accept his answer and moved on to the next 1st District member. Once I had completed talking to everyone in the room, I was still at 10 out of 15 votes from my own district members. I was good with those numbers because if I could get 9 votes from the 7th, I would be all set.

However, it does not look good if a candidate cannot get the total support from their own. I left it alone and continued eating my dinner while watching everyone in the room. There were a lot of conversations going on in the corners of the roomy house. I did not bother to get into any of them. I remained in the living room talking to my absolute supporting member of the District. He was always pleasant, and he did not play games. He would definitely give it to me straight if he was not going to support me. From our previous conversations I could tell he was also disappointed that I was not getting everyone's full support.

The following day, I set my sights on the 7th District. I never like to remind people of what I do or have done for them. I think that it is their responsibility to remember and show gratitude without being told. But when I made a certain call to a member of the 7th, I could not resist telling him that if it had not been for me, he would be nowhere near the HDTC because they did not want him to be a member but some of us at the Tuesday night meeting pushed for him and thus, he got on their slate and won.

Actually, I don't think he had collected one signature other than his own for the slate and he got elected due to the work of myself and others. I was not pleased with him, but I was also not willing to let his vote go, and I parked our conversation in the parking lot.

I know you must be thinking by now; my parking lot was getting pretty crowded. You are right but I need to park what he said and keep it moving. I did not have a lot of time to spend on him. I would come back to him later. I planted the seed I wanted to plant and now I must move on.

I'm not one to carry a grudge, but his comments rubbed me wrong because I know what I had done for him and he had the nerve to be acting brand new. When I asked if he was going to endorse me, he had the nerve to say that he was going to wait and see what the rest of his town committee members are going to do and then he will get back to me. I felt like telling him not to bother, but a vote is a vote, and I was still short of 40 so I could not say what I really wanted to say for the moment. At least that was a possibility and someone in my position right now cannot afford to lose one vote so his comments can stay in the parking lot for now.

However, I was livid. This was an election for town committee that not only had to get signatures, but because they had a challenge slate against them, I and a few more individuals actually had to knock on doors for them, make phone calls and stand outside at the polls, in the cold, to convince people to vote for the slate to which he had been elected.

Needless to say, he was another member of the Tuesday night group I had to pull away from. More and more I kept getting the feeling that this weekly group meeting was a waste of my time and expertise. There seemed to be less and less value for me to continue to meet.

However, I kept thinking I needed to stay so I could at least get some assistance to help me with the constituents I wanted to represent. I felt my time was being wasted because I was doing a lot of helping the people who attended these meetings or those who came for assistance but what I received was no help from them except from the two members who shall remain nameless. Thus, I would attend the meetings but found myself with less and less information to share. I assume they could feel that there was something missing, but they did not ask, and I did not say.

I looked at this as another one of those stumbling blocks I had to get over to get to where I was going. I chalked it up as another lesson learned. I trust that when I gave people my all, I should not have to say a word for them to return some sense of gratitude. Not that I want them to give all I give because we have different knowledge base, but the respect of returning the favor would be nice.

CHAPTER NINE

July 27, 2015 had finally arrived. I must admit I was quite nervous going into the convention. I hadn't talked to my Spokesperson/Campaign Manager for a few hours prior to this moment and, last, we did speak I found out my town committee's support was for me and two others in our district plus two new candidates in another district. This meant I was finally getting their full support along with two other candidates that were in the 7th and they were holding out of the 6th vote for a bargaining chip. Oh, I forgot to mention that each person could cast a vote for 6 candidates no matter what District that candidate was from. This was a convention of the entire HDTC, and we were in the Bulkeley High School Auditorium.

The one thing I could say positively about the 1st District was that they would always support their own on the first round of the voting. If it had to go to a second round, they had already worked that out so that there would be no confusion on the floor of the convention from this district.

Their support for me also meant while I was getting my district's support the other candidates were getting my district's support plus their own who had only promised me the vote of 9 of their 16 members. That did not make me feel good. But finally, I could at least, count to 40 even though one member of my district was holding out and I knew these things could go belly up real fast. I surely did not want a repeat of what happened in 2011.

This was not the easiest of campaigns. My Spokesperson/Campaign Manager was coordinating with other districts about candidates other than myself. I was feeling quite uneasy throughout the process. I kept running into people who would from time-to-time questions if she was still running. I acted as if I knew nothing about the continuation of that.

However, it was always in the back of my mind. I found it quite difficult to whole heartedly trust her. That left me tense throughout the endorsement process. So, in essence what was going on was other candidates had their own campaigns plus my Campaign Manager advocating for them. I kept thinking this could not be a good thing for me.

Nonetheless, here we are at the convention and now there are suddenly several other candidates being nominated from the floor who did not participate in the process. I felt this only further complicated things for me. I was not sure how their inclusion would impact my endorsement. I only knew between me and my Spokesperson/Campaign Manager, we had secured the commitment of 40 HDTC members' votes. I actually received 14 from the 1st and one was still holding out until the end. I hoped she would vote for me too. At this point it was a wait and see moment. She was not talking, and I was not asking again.

So here we are, it is mountain climbing time. And those who refuse to cast their endorsement votes for me the last time we played this game were depended on to cast them this time or I was going to be up for a night of embarrassment along with all of the supporters who accompanied me to the convention.

As always, the convention started out with the roll call. The next is the pledge of allegiance and the prayer. After which all political correctness went to hell in a matter of seconds. The first thing on the agenda was the nominations for Mayor. Here is where it got interesting.

The first person nominated was the sitting Mayor of the City of Hartford, who already knew he was not going to be receiving the HDTC endorsement and he would be considered the challenger. When it came time for the nominees to speak the sitting Mayor, who was not receiving the nomination, rose to say that he was not going through the process of these nominations and he would take his case to the streets and with that, he and several of his supporters walked out of the room along with several town committee members following him. I was hoping they were going to come back because some of them who left with him were votes I desperately needed for my own endorsement.

Next, the endorsed Mayor came to the mike and expressed his appreciation for all who had come to support him, and he thanked the HDTC for their endorsement. After which there was the roll call by district, in alphabetical order and everyone present cast their votes for him and he received more than enough for the endorsement.

Next on the agenda was the Council endorsements. My heart started racing at a fast pace. There were several nominations from the floor for Council candidates. I was amongst them. I called Pastor Troy Moses of Shefa of Grace Church of which I am a member, on the phone, and explained to him the process as it was playing out before me. His response was rewardingly comforting. He said, *"Don't worry. You got this. We are praying for you."*

Actually, the Sunday prior to the HDTC Convention, First Lady preached, and she asked the congregation to picture themselves where they wanted to be. Of course, I pictured myself getting the endorsement, but I was doubtful as it played out because at this moment, I did not see how that was going to come to fruition. I hung up the phone to pay close attention to what was going on. I remembered last time I took my eyes off of the board, my numbers had changed, and I was not aware of how that happened. I was paying very close attention to that board this time. I also asked my supporters to let me know if they noticed any changes while I went down to other districts to advocate for more votes.

When there were no more nominations the HDTC was called upon in numeric order. Of course, the 1st District was first. Each member of our district casts 4 votes and passed on the other 2. The entire 3rd District passed. I sank down in my seat because I had counted 9 votes from the 3rd. To receive none had me really nervous. I think I was breaking out in a cold sweat. The 4th District was next. I received only 4 votes from them. Now I am sweating and recalled my Pastor to explain to him that I am receiving the least number of votes on the board that was being tallied from the stage for all to see.

There was always trouble for me in the 5th District. However, I received my faithful 3 votes. The 6th District was next, and they gave the 4 votes they had promised from the beginning and the 7th District only casted 6 votes. Once the first round ended; there was a motion to recess. The motion was second and passed. Those who received less than 40 votes went to the front of the room.

When I saw this movement, I immediately went to the front of what we called the pit because me and two other candidates were tied at 43. Those who had

47 or more did not bother to come down. I was not taking any chances. I wanted to see who I could talk to, to get ahead of the three way tie I found myself in after the first round.

My Spokesperson/Campaign Manager went to the front of the auditorium also known as the pit to lobby for additional votes. When she came down, I went over to the 7th District and expressed my disappointment. I thought that the majority of them made a commitment to voting for me at the convention. Some of them said they were going to cast their votes for me in the second round. They also had reservation about the 1st District. They wanted to be sure the 1st was going to honor their commitment to endorse their two candidates of which they had given some votes but were also holding out to have some votes to bargain with should the need arise.

Another important fact was that this was also the year the City of Hartford had its First Black Female running for Probate Judge. So, the conversation went something like this: *"If you expect for the 1st to vote for your two candidates and your Probate Judge I need to get those votes."* I was told, not to worry. The votes will be there.

The 7th was sitting next to the 5th but I did not bother myself talking to them because some of their members would never cast a vote for me because they were still mad because around February 2005, when I was first elected and hosted my first Annual Honoring Our Own Reception; a Black History Month event, with my mother Prenzina Holloway and Petrel Maylor my Executive Assistant at the time, a member of their district was arrested the night of the event and the Honoring Our Own Committee advised me to pull her bio and citations from the program just minutes prior to the event starting because that would cause negativity on the program just getting out of the gate. Therefore, I knew not to ask them for their support. I was happy to get the 3 votes I knew I could get.

Having had the conversation with the 7th made it a little better but I was still not above the tie. As I returned to the pit, the two other candidates whom I was tied with were also there. We all started to approach one of the State Representatives that was there to get him to move his people from the 5th District. Before I could finish my conversation with him, Representative Minnie Gonzalez of the 3ʳᵈ District came over to say, *"Don't worry. We got you."*

I felt a lot better, though still nervous. However, one thing I knew for sure, that although many town committee members claim to have issue with Representative Gonzales, one thing I knew was she was a woman of her word. If she said it. She would make it so. That meant the remainder of her town committee members were going to cast their votes for me. She had only one ask of me. She asked that I vote for her candidate for Constable of which being a person of my word I said I would make her candidate one of my four votes for Constable.

No sooner than we had finished talking my Spokesperson/Campaign Manager came over and basically told me to go back to my seat and be a candidate. Surely, I was not listening to that 100% because of the daily events of the past when she was advocating for herself to get the endorsement at this same convention.

However, feeling like I had done all I could do to make my case for more votes for my endorsement I started moving toward my seat. Before I could get to my seat, I felt a tap on my shoulder. It was the newly endorsed candidate for Mayor asking me what else I wanted if I did not get this endorsement.

"You think I did all of that work to include spending the night here at Bulkeley High School until 2am in the morning to leave with nothing? I came for this endorsement," I explained.

He walked away and went to talk to the other two candidates who were in a tie with me. I guess he asked them the same question. I assumed this was his attempt to help the HDTC settle the confusion and move on to the Probate Judge and Constable endorsements.

The chime started. This meant for everyone to return to their seats because the convention was about to reconvene. As always, we started with the 1st District. This time it was a little different. The 1st District gave up the rest of their votes. I still did not get the missing vote from my own town committee member.

The 3rd District, as Representative Minnie Gonzalez had promised, gave 10 of 13 of their votes to me. Of which I said, *"Thank you,"* as I continued to watch the others votes come in.

The 4th gave a few more of their votes. The 5th District was no change. The 6th gave me 9 of their votes and held on to the rest of them. The 7th District only gave 2 more. I got out of my seat and went over to some of their own committee members whom I knew very well and asked them to start subtracting votes from a certain 7th District candidate and instructed them to give their vote to anyone who even if they received their votes would not end up having enough votes to get the endorsement.

So here we go, let the subtraction game began. One by one, they started subtracting their votes from a certain candidate in the 7th District and giving it to another candidate who did not have enough votes to matter.

This happened about three more times before the 7th District started to see one of their candidates' votes slipping away and they started adding votes to my count. Once they started adding to my count the subtractions from their candidate stopped. I again called my Pastor and we prayed over the phone. I informed him that the tied had turned and now I am starting to gain more votes than I needed for this endorsement.

Whew! That was no easy task, and I must admit I learned a lot of lessons about myself and other people. But, most importantly I accomplished my goal. I found some real friends and I got the HDTC endorsement. The rest is history.

When it was all said and done the following are the Official Results of the 2015 Hartford Democratic Town Committee Convention as recorded and reported by the Secretary.

Totals	Top 6 Endorsed											
	55	55	51	49	48	48	44	23	23	22	16	7
	Clarke	Winch	Gale	Thames	Concepcio	Sanchez	Kennedy	Anderson	MacDonaldo	Feliciano	DeeJesus	Espinoza
1ST Assembly District	7	14	15	11	15	8	15	3	0	1	1	0
3RD Assembly District	11	10	11	2	2	10	2	2	11	2	12	0
4TH Assembly District	3	11	11	9	12	8	9	3	0	5	1	5
5TH Assembly District	7	3	6	7	1	0	7	5	0	5	0	1
6TH Assembly District	13	4	3	9	12	13	2	1	9	5	2	0
7TH Assembly District	14	13	5	11	6	9	9	9	3	4	0	1

If you ever decide to climb a mountain, two very important facts to remember; you can always climb higher if you prepare for the trip and dump dead weight.

Printed in the United States
by Baker & Taylor Publisher Services